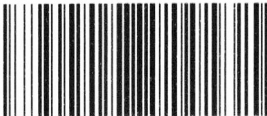

CW01475256

Surviving Love

for Catherine

Mi Eterna Amada

Surviving Love

Kevin Bailey

Published by bluechrome publishing 2005

2 4 6 8 10 9 7 5 3 1

First published in Great Britain in 2005 by
bluechrome publishing
PO Box 109,
Portishead, Bristol. BS20 7ZJ

www.bluechrome.co.uk

A CIP catalogue record for this book is available from the
British Library

ISBN 1-904781-53-5

Kevin Bailey was born and grew up in Wallingford, Berkshire, where he attended the local Grammar School. He was later educated at The University of York and University College, Bath. In 1990 he founded the international literary journal *HQ Poetry Magazine*, which he still edits and publishes independently. He has been closely involved in the work of London's poetry group *Piccadilly Poets* and *The Live Poets Society* in Bath. In 2000 he edited (with Lucien Stryk) the classic anthology *Contemporary Haiku*. Since 2001 he has co-organised and judged at the annual *Poetry on the Lake* festival held at Orta San Giulio in Italy. In 2004 he adjudicated the prestigious Sasakawa Prize for Haikai. His poetry and commentaries have appeared in a wide variety of publications.

Originally trained as a Psychologist, he is now a self-supporting writer and lives in Swindon, Wiltshire, at the heart of his beloved North Wessex countryside, where the ghosts of Hardy's tragic characters still wander.

ACKNOWLEDGEMENTS

Poems in this collection have previously been published in the following magazines : *Brussels Sprout* (US), *Candelabrum, Cicada* (Japan), *Critical Forum* (India), *Envoi, Hummingbird* (US), *Iota, Kitaplik* (Turkey), *Ko Magazine* (Japan), *New Age, North West Literary Forum* (US), *Odyssey, Orbis, Ore, Outposts, Poetry Cornwall, Poetry Nippon* (Japan), *Poetry Today* (India), *South, Staple, The Black Mountain Review, The Honest Ulsterman, The Mainichi Daily News* (Japan), *The SHOp* (Ireland), *The Frogmore Papers, Variations* (Switzerland), *Wallingford Magazine, Woodnotes* (US), and in the anthologies : *Civil Service Poetry* (European Commission Literary Circle), *Star Trek : The Poems* (Iron) and *Haiku for Lovers* (MQP). The translation and re-creation of Sappho's poetic fragments was begun in the warmth, comfort, and encouraging atmosphere of the J. B. Morrell Library at the University of York.

My thanks to my Parents, and the poets Gary Bills and Mike Hogan, for their enduring support and encouragement : my *Clotilde* for loving fidelity to her *Bel-Ami* ; and Hannah and Lawrence for bringing up such a wayward father.

The illustrations are by Catherine Roberts.

CONTENTS

A Treading of Uncertain Ways

A Treading of Uncertain Ways

YERMA : ... the womb holds tender sons the way soft clouds hold rain.

Federico Garcia Lorca

... no hewing out with axes from this delicate place.

A Treading of Uncertain Ways

In the sharp pine-wood she stands among
the slender trunks. His books are dented
with rain-drops. Should he rise and follow
her, or gather words? (*This has always
been his dilemma*). Between two loves ...
Now lost in the dark wood ; no hewing out
with axes from this delicate place. Night
falls. The stars cannot guide him through
this unnatural maze. His love, the search
for lost paths : a treading of uncertain ways.

Fox

Exposing himself from the hedge,
the gargoyled face of a fox ; panting
his shame ; doing the quick-change
to guilty expressions of movement :
skipping off across shit-brown furrows,
satisfied with my shock ; only a back-
ward glance at one who understands.

Tangled Roots

Delicately pink as a baby's mouth
that's satiated with milk, a dribble
of sperm leaks out - a gentle flow -
the uterus pulsing back what it
does not need : the surplus gob
making more wet the stained bed ;
this sexual canvas, bare as our flesh.

Our tangled bodies have pulled up
their tangled roots - we have quenched
them with tales of coital randomness
and past loves : we have brothers and
sisters - in - sex ; an incest of memories
to bless this afternoon of sweat. We are
part of the *great flood*. We are *not* jealous.

The Sixties Thing *for Roger McGough*

Scene One (Profane)

The lamps are covered with red silk
so it's *Hell* in here and the tart I brought
is drunk. A simple strobe ; fag smoke drifting
and the *Stones* beating the *Beach Boys* to a pulp.
Now, astride the joss-stick, she scents her cunt :
a Mogul trick ; but tonight, before sin commingles
with diverse pox, she'll fuck us all, and we, her
lovers, forget the girl, but not the porous stink
of *Gordon's Gin*, and pricks glazed with yoni.

Scene Two (Sacred)

I sit in the college quad and catch sight of a
blue velvet skirt shimmering in sunlight ; her
bird's nest of black hair tumbling over a cheese-
cloth top : brown nipples in obscura : green eyes :
lips puckered up in a thoughtful smirk - *Oh*, first
love, and all those songs about *Cecilia* and *Suzanne*.
I am caught : and summer, autumn and spring
dote on her shape and liberal chat, that we know
will lead to babies turning into ourselves again ...

18

Counting the Clouds

On the red pullover
her lover
is heaping primroses

that avalanche away
from her little
but loving breasts ;

rising and falling,
rising and falling,
with each silent breath.

Across a universe
her steady green eyes
are counting the clouds.

Red Moon

A red moon swims
in the wine glass.

The day has been hot.

Drink *honeysuckle* and
the female scent of stocks.

Lead my feet blind

over the trampled grass
to your *earthy* lair.

Love me.

The night has a fearless air,
and the future,

a touching of *white* flesh.

Pomegranate

She was just so ripe - there is no other
word to describe this fullness of flesh,
breasts, thighs ; round face, and bright
eyes - she was just so ripe, and ready
to burst like the pomegranate, held up,
eclipsing the sun : its light, a trans-
luscent pink - as she is naked ... I bite :
seeds and juice from this little fruit
on my lips, and, as always, afterwards.

The Crying Girl*

On the rock of patience
you sat in the dusk,
trouble-darkened eyes
exposing such pain ;

Written on your lips
the naked emotions,
breaking your soul
sobbing your fate ;

In your mind
thoughts shed tears,
but your tree of life
returned to fruitfulness ;

For your heart's grievings
were silent, and given to
Earth in its wise turning
to the starry heavens.

[*from the Greek of George Seferis]

Sex

With her open legs
she offers up
the shrimp-pink
aqueous
hole

A little worn perhaps
but honest
in its shawl
of matted
hair

*

I intrude,
parting lips
so much sweeter
than are often
kissed

And beyond
licentious flesh
the echo of myself
lives
on

.
.
.

Hairs

I have hairs under the foreskin. Dark,
trapped hairs, there, under the foreskin.
My little *pluckings* from her, pulling at the
skin like wire cutting cheese, as she lay,
dead *plucked*, and recently plucking from me,
the intangible benefits of orgasm and seed.
Taken into her, this short endurance
merchandise ... And yet, here I have her
hair : lasting for a thousand years hair,
trapped under my cell-dying foreskin :
pieces of an ignored *immortality*, privately
stored, for this last reference.

Portrait of Sarah *(In Autumnal Palette)*

By the fire-place ; the fire, and a glow
on your face, breasts bronze at their
tapered ends and your long copper
hair thrown like a cowl over square
shoulders. You sit, prim as a cat,
naked, on your knees, on the mat ;
the glint in your eyes, the straightness
of your back ; pressed haunches, all
an overflow of sculpted flesh softened
in chiaroscuro. The books on every shelf
dancing ; the walls, like Troy, golden.

Italian Observation

Out of the old Italian fountain head -
out of the lion's mouth, this aqua vitae.
The champagne in your mouth dribbles.
You whisper to the man across the table.
He strokes your chin. The water chuckles.

Later, above the square, through the open
balcony window, across the bed where
you are winnowing the first harvest of sex :
the sound of the fountain. Had I spoken,
I'm sure it would have been so different.

The Doll

Why the mask? This pale carnival mask -
fixed smile on ruby lips ; black wig of
Greek curls ; the doll's body too fragile
to handle ... I will play with these limp
arms and legs until their sinews snap -
twist the head into every angle that is
inhuman - drop you, just to hear the
baked china crack - dead eyes fanning
the lashes to a fixed stop ... And then,
with a kind of regret, I will try to mend
all the parts : and in the process, learn
all I can of the doll-maker's art.

The Bath

Louise has filled the white enamel bath. On a
cork-topped stool, a brown paper bag of little
oranges tears open : the floor is scattered with
setting suns. Her clothes have crumpled onto
a chair : salmon pink shift ; yellow cardigan ;
stockings ; a plain pair of briefs ; a cotton
brassière. She pours blue oil from a jar. Sinks
into Aegean warmth ; breasts, *Olympian* above
the foam. She leans forward : sleek shoulders
a seagull cutting the air. From the depths, a
slick of red aborts her *Labyrinthine* tale.

In Paris

i

Cobble stones glacéd. The rain
has sweetened them : sugared
the mood in this Paris street -
the flood ; smooth as silk...

ii

Full gutters piss loudly down
slit-barred drains : fine melody
of a sombre kind ; and wetness
connects with the low hung sky.

iii

Shop lights. The fast bloom
of tearful umbrellas. Under one,
still hidden, I predict her face -
lucid as evening *fleur de lys*...

My Library of Life

My wife, *ma femme*, my library of life :
my books as flesh and flesh as books,
nesting, unalphabeticized, relating only
part to part, subject to subject, a creature
alive ; the whole story in parts, whole, part
of the story of stories and on, ad infinitum
from woman to woman, library to library
remoulded again and again ; the old and
new ; informing, the immortal beloved.

The Black and Green Dress

I asked her (she was reluctant) to put on
the dress for remembrance of younger days.
She put on the dress. A faded black and green
pattern on Indian cloth. A tie at the back,
tightened, that draws the hem to mid-calf
and pulls the waist into a hand's dream -
and the breasts, as they should be, softened.
You wear the dress : nothing, but the dress -
bare feet and arms. Underneath, white flesh.
Only the dress has aged. Time, has always
seemed an irrelevance. Old decoration over
skin, over something, hidden, that is more.

Jam Making

'Afterwards, when both were wives
With children of their own...' *

All along the window sill, the ripening plums
she has placed so carefully with a tender hand :
two lines of fruity *glans* : an unconscious ranking
of her lovers' parts she has counted out for jam -
an aproned *Laura*, murdering songs from those
Goblin years, nervously, as she sweetens her pan ;
forgiving, with every turn of the wooden spoon,
her priapic youth, when fruitful moisture ran.

Much and many the nights warm and dew pearly
she sought the wasting joys of juice and honey...

She would confess : *Fake* virginity, *Mock* love,
the *Dissembled* passions of her marriage bed -
to Daughters ... but *not* the clutching pleasure
Sisters take in latent thoughts of wicked men.

[*Goblin Market* by Christina Rossetti]

Bath Time

In this warm bath
shared with hairy
Agamemnon
and loquacious
Marat
I try to ignore
my vengeful wife
rattling cutlery.

Still Birth

A chaos of clouds scudding through dark eyes.
The hand's descent from forehead, and down
crossing breasts - her triangulation of faith -
fingers lingering to gather sense
from the storm coloured nipples. Silently,
it thunders in her heart : so silently
both beginning and end of touch are forgot.
So plain the emptiness of these human hands -
their miming shape around this loss : the empty,
emptying gesture. Acid tears trickle out ; fall,
and glisten in the lightning's shock, burning
like the jilted child that's slipped her womb -
this nameless lump, damned by some lesser god.
The bruised sky rages, blindly, in our thoughts.

Hare

I found the severed
head of a hare
staring a dry stare

and gobbing flies
in the long grass
by the river.

The passing shiver
of charnel *Nature*
closing tired eyes.

The Scent

He strokes his beard in the crowded street
and is not surprised when from his hand
comes the talisman of one bitter scent :

tested on his tongue, it seems a blend
of lad's love with lavender, his fingers
and clumsy thumb have taken up :

an indistinct flavour, recalling her cries ;
loud as a birth - and now the dilute
of a love he touched, that will not fade.

Titanic

In the cup
this half sunk
tea-bag ;
the Titanic
of our love,
as we sit
in the cafe,
knowing
our talk
has become small
and our feelings
withered ;
and yet,
still unsure
of how to say
good-bye.

Caliban

i

A year later, at the end of another wet August
and frequent meetings in strange places
she came back, body full to bursting
and spread naked on my bed, coveting
more of the same sweat and semen
that had brought all this change into our lives.

ii

Under her belly the child elbowed a plastic
wave across her flesh. His stumpy art pickled
in aspic. The mutated truth of this deceived life
made *sub rosa* for her husband's sake. I baptised
my son ; and she transformed that perfect boy
into a lie's Caliban I cannot hope to mend.

There is a Fine Pear Tree in My Garden*

I can't make sense of *things* anymore. The internal
flaws have shown themselves. There is a drought.
No tears have fallen for months. I have the odd
sympathy. Some *Bach* or *Beethoven* suggests what
I *might* feel, if I had the heart for it. A poetic ennui,
said un-poetically. *Dis*-integration is coming. *Crack!*
The beam above Jason's head - the curse of witches.
The cunts we take to bed - and make mothers of.
Children smothered in the womb. The father abjured.
Once, despite the uncertain bond, a son could fall
with tearful eyes upon his father's neck, for pride or
pity's sake. It's all Greek to me. Why *do* mothers fuck
their sons? And yet, I hold together for better times.
There is a fine pear tree in my garden. I live in hope.

[* '*Now when the steadfast goodly Odysseus saw his father thus wasted
with age and in great grief of heart, he stood still beneath a tall pear tree
and let fall a tear ... And he sprang towards him and fell on his neck
and kissed him ...*' Homer : Book XXIV of *The Odyssey*]

Turning the Corner

I turned the corner. This is a phrase
with other meanings. I got well. I got
solvent. I improved my view of life.
I turned the corner - brick wall
giving way to street? Tall hedge
to bucolic avenue? *I turned the
corner,* and saw the road so many
have imagined ; the described ways
I have seen as a fellow traveller ;
the clichéd *journeys of the mind*
visualised at every turn, however
unexpected, yet still familiar.

Jasmine

There is nothing like the scent of *Jasmine*.
It is the carved saints in lonely churches ;
the voices of lost women ; the sun of youth ;
the hill-path between low hedges ; a first
love never forgotten ; the flesh in moonlight
that turned towards us ; it is death ; the pallid
flower ; the constellations of remembering.

The Magdeburg Maidens

Stone, maidens we presume, standing confused,
with stone maidenheads intact, caressed smooth
by mason's hands who loved them as daughters.

High, on the cathedral front at Magdeburg,
their plaits and little bosoms are fixed,
unable to ripen and balance round hips
that will never bear the weight of love.

At my stare, they each affect a smile,
concerned that I should place their frozen
imago puella on so neat a pedestal.

Only one, with open eyes can read
my thoughts, know I think these girls
that animate such delicate wrists
should live, and hold this new *Pygmalion*.

Cat *for Simone Simon*

You wash so carefully the same place,
rough tongue smoothing the tangled fur,
teeth gnawing at burrs, but not observing,
as do I, the fine dust, cobwebs, and odd
small leaves, gathered on your coat -
the only remaindered clues, the only
dumb explanation of where you've been
since the last tryst in our on-going game
of love and evasion. How I have come
to appreciate this partly joined life :-
my *muse* - my *familiar* : my *Mephisto* wife.

Ecce Homo

1

The poem tasted of sour wine.
He spat it out : slammed doors :
threw books - imagined a fire
that would burn the whole
cursed effort of putting life
(as he saw it) into words ...

2

Long before dawn, he lay
in the garden. At his back
Mother earth, and above ;
the unreachable spill
of the *Via Lactae* - its milk,
richer than any human love.

3

Behold the Man, spinning
in the dark : the light of
the past *netted* in his *not*
unique mind - its outward
start, falling back into the
deeper spaces of himself.

'It Comes, It Comes...' *

The flesh gives out. It must. Skin
giving way to blanched bones.
The private grin of the corpse
in its box, as it settles to dissolution,
resolving to a perfect form, in the ennui
of the grave, or honour of the tomb.

We all ignore Mercutio - embarrassed
by the *Reaper* cutting too soon -
the seasons, moving on, to our own
ripening - remembering the one thing
not lived through, but imagining *it*
in every form, as it rattles by

industrious in its swing of blade -
every time, scything closer ; the blackness
nearer - the *null* place ... *It comes*, it comes
in chilled limbs and failing breath - or
as the shock and pain of an assassin's blade :
it comes ; *darker* than we realised.

[*The last words of John Keats, 1821]

The Widow

The sexy black dress she wears is chic, hitting just
the right stylistic note as a counterpoint to grief.
The morning sun stabs light through the stained
glass window : it ignites her hair into a burning
bush that speaks of her back to be youthful and
alluring in its shape. On both sides, a child cradles
her hips : a neat triptych, standing the strain of
hymns and mawkish valedictions to the dear
departed stiff. She is young, and will make good
the time she's lost to his comfortable neglect.
The last seed falls from the fruit inside her -
his testicles wither, and the dried sex that marked
their sheets has been washed away. A green season
will succeed the creped wreath. Soon, I will comfort
the empty widow - but first : to the happy grave.

The Boat

I rowed over the glass lake in a mist
bellowed from the nose of some hidden beast, far off,
beyond the birds singing in the shadow tops of trees
edging the land - still out of reach.

Water chimed down the oars' edges.
A wake of vortices trod back :
rowlocks clumped with a poetic beat -
I would have been lost,
had not some sense of direction
(part historic ; part ancestral self-myth),
familiar with voyaging beyond the certain
guided my helm.

It's at times like these I know the *Old Gods* live,
and from their unchristian paradise
the past blood still flows within my shriven quick :
the echo sounds to my deepest self - marking the shallows
of that *Other-world* from which I drift ...

Man With a Movie Camera* - *Odessa, 1929*

The empty seats in the Kinema - velvet,
row after row of grey, fall as one rolling wave.
The film is silent on its tracks - cars and trams
glide past shops with Cyrillic signs : the carousel
is unwrapped and turns pretty girls up and down :
the crowds spin : fly-wheels, pistons, and springs
are true to their natural motions - each a slave,
sculpted to enslave - steel never looking better,
than in its black and white costume ...

This comforting testament where even mono -
chrome smoke and grime, vagrants, empty parks
and the poor in lines, are beautiful. Behind this
revolution ; this mute change, a music so loud
that it cannot break the silence of the clicking film.

[*A silent film by Dziga Vertov with live music performed by
The Michael Nyman Band at St George's Hall, Bristol on the
26th. September, 2003]

The Love-Song of Zefrem Cochran*

The shadow of the bird has marked the wall,
blackened my face, drawn the eyes of the
stranger ever closer, and I am afraid for the
dark is behind and the red wave of evening is
crashing down. The darkness has come to
claim the turning away ; the turning half of all
I am, and ever will be : this blue O the world
stage from which we fly, and dip a toe in star-
light. The roar of flight ; the rush of distance
come, dashing over the edge of time. The face
of *God* is masked in shame. We out-stride our
Maker, and have arrived, never the same again.

Our craft has found your beauty. A sperm to
ovum. The opiate aired curve we ride to. Invade
its virgin mist, and twist to land. There are met
by a white star's rising and a dewed green that
wets bare feet. As we alight - the smaller step is
hers. Mine is a great leap that takes me nowhere.
There is a moon under which something pulls
like a spider's web or the slackened strings of
the *Aolean* harp - like plain-song in empty space.
The first night we are *Adam* and *Eve*, and with
the first light I awake to find a monster, or wiser
being, has taken the guts of my sleeping friend.
I recall her last words ; 'This is going to be fun ...'
and cast what I loved into our quantum fire.

The rain outside is making the grass greener, and
the pale cheeks of remembered friends a delusion,
when choosing raindrops, or tears as the most
eloquent metaphor for grief. She is our first dead :
the queen and mother of this new world ; the un-
leaven saviour of our cynical faith. Alone again, the
Vitruvian man does somersaults like a *Harlequin* ;
his mad hands and feet grasping at their full extent,
the limits, the very edge. So she went into Heaven -
that is all we comprehend ; the figures do not add
up ; the theories are always flawed and *God* still
laughs behind the proscenium arch.

[*The Tau Ceti System - May, 2071]

50

Mars Trip   *for Sir Patrick Moore at Eighty*

Speed, denied the sensual grip of wind
and ocean, unbucked by waves, straight
as an arrow, the ship's tip, aimed at *Ares*
leaves only a wake of Euclidean lines.

The smell of honeysuckle. From this little
plastic phial, a June evening tries to deny
the existence of steel bulkheads and
sterile air. He floats, eyes closed, within
the chrysalis of hope : the stars are steady ;
the remote *Earth* a crackle of insect static.

Day-dreams come more frequently now :
the unrequited love of green and blue -
his arms embrace an entire world.
Homer's poem enchants from disk :
the fibril siren-song on every sense
that seeks the touch of home and love.

Bound safely in his memories, he makes
this long return to an old beginning.
No hubris strides his brave new world ;
he knows his place, and stands in awe
of the journey made, Odysseus-like.

Outside

Outside
a foot-fall
on the pavement

some high
heeled laughter
and a silence –

a kiss?
The pushing desire
to know …

We must resolve
not to be
confronted by
realities –

to confuse
our story

to allow
those strangers in
who would romanticize
our world.

Arthur and Amélie
Eight Scenes from The Natural History of Love

*It only needs a very small quantity of hope to beget love.
Even when hope gives way to despair after a day or two,
love will persist.*

Stendhal

The flesh yields like dough.

Scene 1

A Solitary Boy

In the church, a solitary boy
practising *cantata* - his notes
                    skittering
among the old rafters. The dangling bell-pulls.
The oscillating ropes.
In the heavy air, a *Magdalena* has undressed.
Plaster white breasts
                    rubbing
through a chemise of dull blue paint.
She steps down from her plinth. Shakes
her hair. Gold flakes
                    in a shaft of light.
A voice, breaking.

Scene 2

Amélie

The sea of waiting, like the breasts of Amélie
are sucked dry by the boy's imaginings ;
  this little *Arthur*
              who has no time -
out of the mind comes eternal life. Dark words
in a milk sea. The boat of paper ; a *Hermes*
along the gutter, to the drain, to the sewer,
to the river - and on, to an ocean where only
Zeus as sun, and eyes beyond a mortal horizon
read.

Scene 3

Man and Girl

In her black coat and green dress
she stands among the bluebells.
Sunlight still makes it through the trees.
A young smile. Hands in pockets.
Unable to resist him
                    the man's hands
draw out two white breasts, like eggs
stolen from a nest. They can be crushed.
It is a crime. He puts them back. Nipples
skiffle down the withdrawing knuckles.
She turns. He will be back. The path is set.
Twilight fades to black.

Scene 4

Christian

The clematis has pushed a pale twine of leaf
through the old window frame. He notices this
as she holds his weighty scrotum like a bag of
gold coin. He is resigned. Calm, despite the theft
that she intends to make. He has no cloak or shirt
to give. No other things to heap upon her. Love
he can give. Forgiveness. The plant has lost its way.
Will cling to anything. Her fingers are climbing.
The grip tightening. The pleasure, moving.

Scene 5

Epiphany

Her small narrow buttocks :
like an uncluttered boy, press upward.
Her breasts are smothering the white sheets.
Her hair is an exhausted blackbird
and her slim legs
                    unicorns chained in flight.
Her anus is a purple star
                              and her cunt
the baby's eye, part awake
                              part in slumber -
puffed, not fully shut ; reacting
to the sun's light ;
                    opening up.
The wet epiphany that marks her life.

Scene 6

A Well Known Stranger

All day alone. Glass, the sun, and an
unresponsive telephone
                            keeping her
convented within the almost sacred smell
of waxed furniture, and the frustrated
ritual of wandering upstairs
to the neatly made bed.
                            She opens a window.
In her breast a pain. The sound of bird song.
A desire to be naked and warm.
                            Time
passes. From a mirror, the chance glimpse
of a well known stranger.
                            Spring
arouses her, although nothing has changed.

Scene 7

Eve

Marching on into you
                    all the new men -
all the men of your dreams. The future highway.
The stars gleam in the water of your eyes.
The flesh yields like dough.
The plump rounding moon
                    is tethered inside.
You rise up. Somnambulist, out of the wifely bed.
Sweat glistens all over your body.
The conjugal seed seeps.
A disorderly queue of *Herms* await your pleasure.
Much will be new.
                    You will savour it like honey.

Scene 8

La Vita Nuova

A bee hovers over her nipple.
She does not move.
                          Her lover watches.
A spill of yellow pollen has rained down
under the beating wings. A small shadow
is targeting her heart.
                          The nipple swells
and slowly rises.
                      Around her hips, the rippled
blue dress is tight. She moves a little.
Breasts swim to find their own level
                              as she sits.
The bee has gone. She has made up her mind.
Cornflowers and poppies
                    catch her eye.
She has more now than the man can give.

Freud's Graffiti

Open and close the beautiful windows
Hung from the day's lips

André Breton

… a breeze risen ghost

Freud's Graffiti

epic poem :
        lost
at sea

nature poem :
        green
as grass

war poem :
        grave
men

sex poem :
        moist
parts

love poem :
        warm
embrace

last poem :
        God
revealed

Air and Water Triptych

I

Blue

the shortest poem
the wistful hue

II

The sun's not quite
in the stream.

Snaking over sandy
fish deserts

The dapple-green
water weeds ...

III

The boys
are bathing naked -

On your timid breast
this pink rose.

Corn Field

The fly-flecked Moon,
tatter grey,
plugs the stretched blue
summer sky
        tight :

A nipple of white
on the night-side breast
of embracing God.

Listen.
There are tunes
of unbound love
in the rustling twilight ...

Earth and Fire Triptych

I

In the copse ; no sound,
except the sniffing of the dog
and the anger of fallen elms.

II

Second pipe -
from my lungs the little whisper
of mutating cells.

III

This child's gravestone
such a little thing
hidden in tall grasses.

Rose-hips

Rose-hips
swollen red amphora

made of things
greener
than God's fingers

jostling for sun
in a swell of
noon wind

spread from the wreck
of a greying oak

Yerma

Gathering the scent of almond blossom
on this still, moonlit, March night ;
I remember you, and the slight curve
of your flank, and the fresh smell
of white flesh pressed by my weight -
in a depth of sheets met, this odour
of love made then - and here, a breeze
risen ghost ; the affect of cursed body
and sense, that knows itself, yet aches :
growing satiate - but incomplete.

'Walking Tom's' Ghost

Chalk dust on her feet from the Downland path -
the perfect imprints, left by cornflowers,
blue as the sky ; blue as her eyes, that look away
from the nearby sounds of harvesting.

How far ahead she always walks - brown legs
and slender hips leading the beast.
The first autumn rain will erase her steps :
her shadow, grown long into the past.

Spring Pastorals

I

White light after rain.
Our hands spread on cold sheets.
Spring is cruel again.

II

Apple tree - April sun
seeping through cracks in my
brown leather shoes.

III

At the wood's edge,
wild flowers, strangled
by the wind :

And among them,
your face, smiling
like a child.

Summer Pastorals

I

White clouds
drift
between her breasts.

II

Her back,
freckled
like a field of brown poppies.

III

Sunset,
our faces turning
slowly orange.

IV

God's nail
scratches
at the Moon.

Autumn Pastorals

I

Dried in the flames of
this amber season - the pale
face of chamomile.

II

My hair still falling :
by the *Way*, a confusion
of drying grasses.

III

Cast high
            a child's voice
        mingling
with the caw of crows
in the Autumn ash.

Purple Lips

I

I rise to meet her :
almost gone within dark clouds
the scarlet sunset.

II

Coal black the piled mat
of hair ; here in my hand, and
there, padding my way.

III

The purple lips
of my black-haired cat suck gently
on a little mouse.

'Superman' Triptych

Superman (Adolf)

Over the high mountains   over wood-framed houses
and Gothic cities   following tram lines
the shadow of wings   and *that man*
in chiaroscuro   smiling
waving   at the window
below   racing ground
and little people   waving back
mouthing   to strains of
Strauss   and Wagner
Oh Superman   *we love you so ...*

Superman II (Edvard)

Somewhere else   Oslo perhaps
by his bed   thin and frail

Edvard Munch   has caught a chill

and stares   and stares

his canvas   half to death
reflecting   what it means
to paint   unloved.

Superman III (Ezra)

perhaps Pound   was right
about Usury   and all that stuff
re. *Commerce*   and the *Unenlightened*
fucking up   the artist's life.

S/F Koan

This denizen
of the Red planet

this mutated
creature

tall
and frail boned

in silk toga
among

the capitols
and columns

of this
new Rome

looks
to the pale twilight

and sees
the old home

an iota
of fractured blue.

For All Time

The bluebells are dying back.
Going out of focus under a fresh
leaf haze. On the moss, her small
white breasts glow in half naked-
ness, appropriate to the season ...

Only pale windflowers and red
campion lounge this close to
the earth. Her dark hair sweeps
shadows through debris made
by this old wood-land space.

Dew clear, her green eyes reflect
bent branches, elongated clouds
and a deeper sky than I would see
if I fell back, mock-dead, into an
open grave that was closing up ...

Love that has trudged this far
can seem uncoiled, seed-spent,
dead perhaps - or just *resting* ;
a silent hiatus to gather breath,
reanimate and seem, *for all time.*

Wasp

A dead wasp
clings to my copy
of Baudelaire.

How appropriate
that this vicious,
foetal thing

should expire
on these
sickly flowers.

Two Love Notes for your Pillow

1 *Sunset*

I did not look, you gave it to me -
that sight of your freckled breasts :
bats flown in the shaded green cave
of your dress, welling up to the light,
forming in my mind, the child I would
nestle there ; in love, for love's sake ...

2 *Sunrise*

The Cyclops dawn studies with one
engorging eye, the eaten man ;
the chewed-up, spat out soul that pens
a meaning to his life by night,
and sleepless crawls to morning's light
with hopes of art in tired bones.

Sappho : Surviving Love

*The love of the Aeolian girl still breathes,
and her hot passions, entrusted to the lyre, still live*

Horace

for Hannah

... behold Lady Dawn spreading her golden tresses

A Prayer to Aphrodite [1]*

Immortal Aphrodite, bright daughter
of the brightest God, I beg you,
do not break my heart, but come to me
as in times past,

when my cries echoed in your father's
house and you came, sparrow-drawn
across the brown earth, to flutter
over my troubled head ...

Reveal your laughing face : ask me again
*'What is it this time Sappho? What does your
heart desire? Who must I entrance to quench
the fire of your passion?*

*Be patient : she that runs away will soon pursue.
She that is spoilt with gifts will give all - and
if she does not love - she shall, and fall
into your arms ...'*

That is my prayer : my sacred wish.
Be my champion Aphrodite, save me,
from this tension of heart
and flesh...

[*The numbers in square brackets correspond with the fragment
numbers given to the original texts of Sappho's poetry in the Loeb's
Greek Lyric 1 throughout.]

The Trap   [168b]

Moonlight fades ;
the Pleiades tumble ... waiting
  half a night ;
  caught in the trap
  of time's passing :
Thus it is, I lie alone.

Our Sacred Grove [2]

She hithers from Crete to the holy temple ;
this strong-branched grove of apple trees
where blossom burns like incense in the sun
and a fragrant mist lifts from the earth -

and where the chill voice of trickling water
whispers through apple boughs, and young roses
cover the ground : through dappled leaves
the scent-infused sleep of nature drips down.

In the pastures horses gallop, pressing by hoof
the wild spring flowers : a wind carrying their
crushed perfume to our sacred grove - follow
trails of sweet breezes...

Now you are here Cypris, take down the pitcher
and fill our sun-drenched cups with nectar :
draw wine-woven air from this our festive place
and be absorbed with us.

Broken Dreams [63]

Morpheus
you enter me
on the blackest nights

and leave me toying
with the shards of dreams
I wanted whole ...

Apple Gathering [105a]

Moonraking ; an apple
on the highest bough
  ripens,
        blushingly,
  like a shy maiden,
  hanging beyond the
Gatherer's reach,
  only to be plucked
  by the bravest hand.

Dew [73a]

The night has gone :
  again *Aphrodite*
has us whispering
  in the dew.

The Beast [130]

Limb-spreading love
shakes me ;
the bitter-sweet,
all conquering
beast ...

In Love [31]

Godlike the man who mirrors you - hears
honey-sweet words and pulsating laughter
from your lips : how fast that sets my heart
a-racing ;

a moment's glance at your beauty and my
mouth is sealed and my tongue broken.
All at once my skin burns, eyes fail, ears
close, sweat flows :

I shake with love's fever and pale like hay -
I'm sure that I will die ; but all can be endured,
though you still prefer this poor man's *passion*
to a woman's *love* ...

Night Long [23]

Amongst mortal women
Hermione, you are most like
the golden-haired Helen.

With you, night long,
my freed heart would
wander dewy banks ...

I Rejoice for You [22]

The *Winterfaced* Gongyla
  is beautiful :
Sing Abanthis of your desire -
Stroke your lyre as you would
  the cloth that covers her breasts :
I rejoice for you ;
I envy your youth ...

Surrender Sorrow [6]

Go - and behold *Lady Dawn*
spreading her golden tresses :
Unplait your fate, and surrender
sorrow to the new day ...

The Garlanded [81]

Dica, weave plaits of wild flowers
through the hayfield of your hair,
and with delicate fingers twist shoots
of dill together, for the *Charites* bless
only the garlanded, and turn away
from the unadorned.

Country Girl [57]

So Andromeda, you've fallen
for that teat-pulling Amazon
of a country girl ...

for heavens sake,
she hasn't even the wit to lift
her smock above her ankles ...

I Forbade It [71]

Mica, I forbade it,
yet still you befriend
the women of Penthilus :

Perfidian, aren't our songs
as sweet as the nightingale,
and theirs as shrill as the wind?

A Warning to Doricha   [15]

Aphrodite of Cyprus ; of the seas,
bring my brother home, humbled
but with gold.

And warn Doricha not to boast
his coming a second time, to wallow
in their way-ward love.

To Doricha [7]

Doricha, *dear*,
don't be stupid -
if you do not come
I shall think you as *arrogant* as a man ...

A Prayer for my Brother's Safe Return [5]

Cyprian Aphrodite and the fifty sea nymphs
keep my brother safe on the water-way home,
and allow, that his heart's desires come true...

Let him atone for his past sins
and become a better friend to those he loves,
who, forgiving, will love him by return -
and let those that did our family wrong,
disappear, and never cause us grief again.

Grant me, Goddess, that a page has turned
and he will bring honour to his sister
and banish all the pain he gave.

Your Friends [3]

Your *fine* and *noble* friends
annoy me beyond sufferance -

Do not reproach me for
'filling out' - you've had your *'fill'*

And I understand the *putridity*
of other minds...

Leaving [94]

I wish I were dead. She's left me crying.
Leaving she said ; 'What misfortune has
been ours, Sappho - I go because I must'.

And I said ; 'Go, be well ; but remember me,
and how we have cared for you - and don't
forget the good times we've had ... and those

many posies of violets, roses and garlands
we've hung about your soft neck, and how,
side by side I've smelt that queenly scent

that is your own - and on our cushioned beds
your desires have been satisfied, tenderly ...'

When You Die [59]

Foolish woman, wealth won't save you
from the grave. When you die, you'll just
rot away, for without serving the Muses
there will be no memory of your name -
nor grief - and even in the domain of
Aides you'll go unseen, in endless drift,
through the blackening corpses ...

A Poem for Anactorias   [16]

Some say, the *élan* of cavalry : some, the shield line -
and yet others that the sea-speeding galleys
are the most beautiful sight on this black earth -
but *I* say, it's what ever you love ...

That's clear enough, surely? For even the 'perfect'
Helen abandoned her family for the love of a Trojan :
deserted her own child without a backward thought
in favour of *'love-blind'* wanderings.

I can't stop thinking about our banished Anactorias -
I'd rather hear the gentle tread of her measured footsteps,
or see that radiant face break to a smile,
than behold all the armed horse and foot of Lydia.

Atys [49]

I loved you, Atys, in times past ...

The Lydian [96]

Often her thoughts turned to you,
blessed you, and rejoiced in your songs.

You were her Goddess,
and now she alone of Lydian women,
like the blushing Moon at sunset

absorbs the stars and casts her light
across salt sea and weed field alike ...

Honey-dew falls on roses ; the frail
thyme and melitot clover ...
In her coming and going she remembers

gentle Atthis, and her heart is torn,
and her sweet breasts heave with sighs.

Daughter [132]

Among the gold-topped flowers
my bright child plays ; dear Kleis ;
  daughter,
  to me you are worth more
  than the greatest kingdom.

The Nymph   [62]

Hiding behind that laurel tree
in the sweet-aired twilight, you sang,
shyly, to the passing girls -

A rare voice from a loving heart ;
but you were here first, so join us now -
an unbound *Daphne* dressed like a nymph.

To Kleis [98]

As a girl, grandma often bound
her dark sea-blown tumbles of hair
with purple riband -

for then it was the height of fashion :
but for you *Kleis*, with hair yellower
than torch-light,

a clutch of sweet-smelling flowers
is quite enough, and finer than any
headband from Sardis ...

Spring [136, 118, 104b, 4]

i

Hopeful messenger of Spring ;
the lovely-voiced Nightingale.

ii

Now, sacred Lyre, speak to me
in a voice that is your own.

iii

O Hesperus,
you are the gentlest
of evening stars.

iv

My spirit is full
when your face
reflects my love.

To the Virgins [30]

Into the virgins, all night long
the love songs of the *nightingale*,
arousing dreams
of a bride's mauve robes ...

Bestir yourselves girls - get the
young bachelors to your beds -
and sing louder, and sleep less,
than that honey-voiced bird.

At the Altar   [54, 103b, 53]

i

Eros has come from heaven
clothed in a purple mantle ...

ii

Into the Chamber
came the bride
on beautiful feet.

iii

So come the rose-limbed Charites -
the daughters of God ...

Love [46, 47, 138, 117a]

i

To the seductive swelling of cushions
I cast my foolish limbs.

ii

Love shakes my heart ;
just as the wind through
mountain oaks.

iii

Stand erect my love ;
let the divinity of your eyes
fall upon me.

iv

Your love
is a smooth doorway.

Selene [154, 34, 168c]

i

Around the altar we gathered ;
Watching Selene in her fullness.

ii

Stars about the Moon
are lost from view -

on all sides the crowds
are *outshone* by her beauty.

iii

The Earth
is embroidered with flowers ...

To a Young Friend   [121, 122, 82a, 126]

i

Dear youth ;
  beloved friend, find the bed
  of a younger woman, for I will not
live with you - I cannot suffer
  being your elder ...

ii

I saw a delicate girl gathering flowers.

iii

Mnasidika is more rounded
than the delicate Gyrinno.

iv

Bind yourself in sleep
to the delicate breasts
of a young mistress.

Delicacy [58]

From the breasts of the Muses
I have sucked great gifts - to sing ;
to play the lyre well : children and
lovers attending
                    but now that age
has papered my skin and whitened
black tresses
                    I cannot be as nimble
as the young fawns, but am ageless
                    for I have loved
Delicacy - and delicate love
has brought me the bright dazzle
and beauty
                    of a sun-filled life.

Temper? [120, 131, 37, 146]

i

But anyone can see I don't have
a nasty temper -
thou *knowest* my gentle heart ...

ii

Atthis, now you think hatefully of me
and fly off to pretty Andromeda.

iii

Chastiser,
let winds and sorrows
carry you off!

iv

I want
neither the sweetness of honey,
nor the stinging of bees.

Confusions [51, 107, 52, 41]

i

Not knowing what to do ;
thoughts run both ways.

ii

Why, in my prime,
do I still long for
my lost maidenhead?

iii

Even with my arms outstretched
I cannot touch the sky.

iv

Dear,
I have known you too long
for my thoughts to change.

In Old Age [21, 44b, 42]

i

In old age,
even though Aphrodite prefers the young,
I will take my lyre
and sing her songs ...

ii

Muses bless us ;
Charites help us;
but still we fume
at being mortal.

iii

The faithful pigeons
cold at heart
loose their wings ...

The Evening Star [104a]

The evening star
gathers all : nets
the old Dawn's
scatterings ; brings
sheep from the hills,
goats from the orchard,
brings sleepy children
to their mother's breast.

Surviving Love [88]

Desire little : know yourself ;
Love as long as you have breath,
  and above all, be a friend ...
Do this, and love is powerless
  to wound.

Adieu   [150, 100, 147, 134]

i

There should be
no lamentations
in the house of a poet -
That is not our way.

ii

And at her death
they covered her
in soft linen.

iii

You know,
someone will remember us,
in a time to come.

iv

I spoke in a dream
with Aphrodite of Cyprus ...

Epilogue : Hector and Andromanche [44]

Aphrodite of Cyprus has sent Idaeus, the messenger,
to tell Greece and all Asia of Hector's eternal fame :

'He brings bright-eyed and graceful Andromanche across salt sea
from sacred Thebe and rich Placia -
and in his ships there are gold bands and bridal gowns highly scented,
and cups of silver, and trinkets and ivory'.

Thus he spoke : and Priam, the hero's father, rose up
and sent word throughout the whole city to all his kin.

... And without delay, mule waggons crowded with
women and shapely ankled girls, set out for Ilium,
joined by the chariots of unmarried bucks and the
proud daughters of Priam ...
                            led by pipes, lyres and rattles -
and virgins singing hymns - all echoing to the sky and Gods ...

The streets were spiked with scent and spices , and old women
set up a joyful wailing - and the men - a chant to skilled Apollo
in supplication he compose a lyric song for their god-like hero :
Hector, and his loyal wife, Andromanche.

AFTERWORD

Half a millennium after her death, Tullius Laurea, the freedman of Cicero, said; 'no day will ever dawn that does not speak the name of Sappho, the lyric poetess'. Even by the first century BC she was a classic, and now, two millennia later, she is still with us, catching hearts. If Homer is the father of Western poetry, then Sappho, who taught us to sing of love, beauty, and passion, is the mother. She is the first woman of Western literature - and yet we know so little about her. According to the classical authors Sappho was born at Mytilene on the Greek island of Lesbos around the year 630 BC. Her father was the merchant Scamander and her mother, Kleis. She had three brothers; Erigyius, Larichus and Charaxus - all of whom seem to have woven trade, politics, and the love of women into the fabric of their complex lives. Sappho grew up to be a short, plain, and dark complexioned woman; this was obviously to the taste of the wealthy merchant Cercylas of Andros, who married her and with whom she had a yellow-haired daughter named Kleis. Sometime later Sappho seems to have decided to live apart from her husband, and by the 42nd. Olympiad (612-608 BC) she had become famous as a composer and performer of love poems and pagan hymns.

Her mastery of poetry and music attracted students, and for the remainder of her life she was the 'Principal' of an academy of younger women - aspiring performers - drawn to her from all parts of the Greek world. Her own poetry reveals the love and passion she felt for some of her pupils, and their names; Gongyla, Anactorias, Dica, and the others, are now immortal. She died, either in her prime by suicide after a doomed love affair, or as an honoured old woman, loved by all. Her own reference to ageing in the poems suggests the latter to be true. After two and a half thousand years, fate and time have so eroded the body of her works that only a few fragments remain of the nine ancient volumes collected by the Alexandrians - and these fragments so incomplete, that in poetic terms, she is almost lost to us - but what has survived in these fractured poems is a human spirit so strong that it can still speak with a living voice. She is the first 'ordinary' woman we can - on the evidence of her own writing - describe as a 'complete' woman; wise, independent, proud, and unafraid to love.

For twenty years I have been travelling back to Sappho in my imagination. It has been a long distance affair, but I think we have grown to understand each other. Carrying the poetic images, metaphors and colloquialisms of her own age, I have welcomed her into my mind and have transmuted them, as incorruptibly as I can, into ours. It is a love-gift to a woman at the other end of time. It is a love-gift to a woman of our and all time.

Easter 1984 to January 2004